GALLUP GUIDES FOR YOUTH FACING PERSISTENT PREJUDICE

Muslims

GALLUP GUIDES FOR YOUTH FACING PERSISTENT PREJUDICE

- Asians
- Blacks
- Hispanics
- Jews
- The LGBT Community
- Muslims
- Native North American Indians
- People with Mental and Physical Challenges

GALLUP GUIDES FOR YOUTH FACING PERSISTENT PREJUDICE

Muslims

Ellyn Sanna

Mason Crest

Mason Crest
370 Reed Road
Broomall, Pennsylvania 19008
www.masoncrest.com

Printed and bound in the United States of America.

First printing
9 8 7 6 5 4 3 2 1

ISBN-13: 978-1-4222-2462-5 (hardcover series)
ISBN-13: 978-1-4222-2468-7 (hardcover)
ISBN-13: 978-1-4222-9341-6 (e-book)
ISBN-13: 978-1-4222-2477-9 (paperback)

Library of Congress Cataloging-in-Publication Data

Sanna, Ellyn, 1957-
  Gallup guides for youth facing persistent prejudice. Muslims / by Ellyn Sanna.
    p. cm.
  Includes bibliographical references and index.
  ISBN 978-1-4222-2468-7 (hardcover) -- ISBN 978-1-4222-2462-5 (series hardcover) -- ISBN 978-1-4222-9341-6 (ebook) -- ISBN 978-1-4222-2477-9 (paperback)
 1. Muslims--United States--Juvenile literature. 2. Islam--Juvenile literature. 3. Prejudices--Juvenile literature. 4. Religious discrimination--Juvenile literature. 5. Religious tolerance--Juvenile literature. I. Title. II. Title: Muslims.
  E184.M88S36 2013
  305.6'97073--dc23
                              2012017109

Produced by Harding House Publishing Services, Inc.
www.hardinghousepages.com
Interior design by Micaela Sanna.
Page design elements by Cienpies Design / Illustrations | Dreamstime.com.
Cover design by Torque Advertising + Design.

Thank you to Anan Ameri and the Arab American National Museum for their generous help with the creation of this book.

CONTENTS

1. Prejudice and Muslims............................ 7

2. A History Lesson.................................. 19

3. Real-Life Stories................................. 33

4. Fighting Prejudice............................... 43

Find Out More....................................... 59

Glossary... 60

Bibliography.. 62

Index.. 63

About the Author................................... 64

CHAPTER 1

Prejudice and Muslims

The root word of prejudice is "pre-judge." Prejudiced people often judge others based purely on their religion, race, or ethnic group; they make assumptions about others that may have no basis in reality. They believe that if your faith is different, or you speak a different language, or you have a different color skin, then they already know you are not as smart, not as nice, not as honest, not as valuable, or not as moral as they are. One group of people that have been the target of prejudice are

Muslims. Prejudice against Muslims is a big issue today, in North America and around the world. Fear of and prejudice against Muslims is called Islamophobia.

WHO ARE MUSLIMS?

Muslims are people who follow Islam, a religion that grew from some of the same roots as Judaism and Christianity. "Islam" means "submission to God," and Muslims try to let God shape all aspects of their lives. They refer to God as Allah; their holy

The Muslim holy book, the Qur'an

scriptures are called the Qur'an, and they consider the Prophet Muhammad to be their greatest teacher.

Just like there are different kinds of Christians in the world, there are also different kinds of Muslims. Some Christians are **conservative** and some are **liberal**, and the same is true of Muslims. Both Christians and Muslims can be fundamentalists. This means they want to get back to the fundamentals—the basics—of their religions. However, their definition of what's "fundamental" is not always the same as it is for other people who call themselves Christian or Muslim.

Generally speaking, fundamentalist Muslims are afraid that the influence of Western morals and values will be bad for Muslims. They believe that the laws of Islam's holy books should be followed literally. Some are willing to kill for their beliefs—and some are willing to die for them as well. Men and women who are passionate about these beliefs have taken part in violent attacks against Europe and the United States. They believe that terrorism will make the world take notice of them, that it will help them fight back against the West's power. Fundamentalist Muslims were responsible for the terrorist attacks on the United States on September 11, 2001, and they have been responsible for other attacks around the world.

But most Muslims are not terrorists. In fact, most Muslims are law-abiding and hardworking citizens of the countries where they live. Some Muslims, however, believe that women should have few of the rights that women expect in most **Western** countries. This makes tension sometimes between conservative Muslims and the people who support women's rights.

But not all Muslims are so conservative and strict. Many of them believe in the same "golden rule" preached by all major religions: "Treat everyone the way you want to be treated."

Despite this, hate crimes against Muslims are increasing across North America and Europe. These crimes range from death threats and murder to more minor assaults, such as spitting, name-calling, and defacing Muslim places of worship. Prejudice against Muslims is a major problem in many parts of the world today.

WHAT CAUSES PREJUDICE?

Why do human beings experience prejudice? **Sociologists** believe humans have a basic tendency to fear anything that's unfamiliar or unknown. Someone who is strange (in that they're not like us) is scary; they're automatically dangerous or inferior. If we get to know the strangers, of course, we end up discovering that they're not so different from ourselves.

They're not so frightening and threatening after all. But too often, we don't let that happen. We put up a wall between the strangers and ourselves. We're on the inside; they're on the outside. And then we peer over the wall, too far away from the people on the other side to see anything but our differences. Then we end up resorting to something called stereotyping.

STEREOTYPES

A stereotype is a fixed, commonly held idea or image of a person or group that's based on an oversimplification of some observed or imagined trait. Stereotypes assume that whatever is believed about a group is typical for each and every individual within that group. "All blondes are dumb," is a stereotype. "Women are poor drivers," is another. "Gay men are **effeminate**" is yet another, and "All Muslims are terrorists" is an especially dangerous stereotype.

Many stereotypes tend to make us feel superior in some way to the person or group being stereotyped. Not all stereotypes are negative, however; some are positive—"black men are good at basketball," "gay guys have good fashion sense," or "Asian students are smart"—but that doesn't make them true. They ignore individuals' uniqueness. They make assumptions that may or may not be accurate.

What's the Difference Between Arabs, Middle Easterners, and Muslims?

- "Arab" refers to a person who speaks an Arabic language. Sometimes it is also an ethnicity, meaning that Arabs tend to share a common ancestry. Arabs come from a certain region of the world. Arab countries include Egypt, Iraq, Saudi Arabia, and Syria, because Arabic is spoken there. People from northern Africa are also called Arabs, but they don't necessarily have the same ancestry as ethnic Arabs.

- A "Middle Easterner" is someone from the area of the world called the Middle East. It partly overlaps with the Arabic world. But it doesn't include any part of Arab Africa. It does include several countries that don't speak Arabic, like Iran.

- "Muslim" refers to someone who practices Islam. There are lots of Muslims in most Arabic and Middle Eastern countries. But Muslims live in other countries too. There are also people of different (or no) religions in Arabic countries. Large numbers of Jews and Christians also live in the Arab region.

In today's world, some people have hurtful stereotypes of Muslim people. They think that all Muslims are the same, when in fact, there are many Muslim countries, and many different kinds of Muslims around the world. Each group of Muslims practices their religion a little differently.

Many of our current stereotypes about Muslims have to do with violence and terrorism. "All Muslims are terrorists," "All Muslims hate the United States," and "All Muslims hate

Do these children look like terrorists?

High School Stereotypes

The average high school has its share of stereotypes—lumping a certain kind of person together, ignoring all the ways that each person is unique. These stereotypes are often expressed with a single word or phrase: "jock," "nerd," "goth," "prep," or "geek." The images these words call to mind are easily recognized and understood by others. But that doesn't mean they're true!

women" are dangerous stereotypes. And they're not accurate. Some people think that all Muslims are Arabs. In fact, most Muslims are not Arabic or even from the Middle East. They live in places like Indonesia or India, or other countries.

We can't help our human tendency to put people into categories. As babies, we faced a confusing world filled with an amazing variety of new things. We needed a way to make sense of it all, so one of our first steps in learning about the world around us was to sort things into separate slots in our heads: small furry things that said *meow* were kitties, while larger furry things that said *arf-arf* were doggies; cars went

Group Pressure

Why do people continue to believe stereotypes despite evidence that may not support them? Researchers have found that it may have something to do with group pressure. During one experiment, seven members of a group were asked to state that a short line is longer than a long line. About a third of the rest of the group agreed that the short line was longer, despite evidence to the contrary. Apparently, people conform to the beliefs of those around them in order to gain group acceptance.

vroom-vroom, but trains were longer and went *choo-choo*; little girls looked one way and little boys another; and doctors wore white coats, while police officers wore blue. These were our earliest stereotypes. They were a handy way to make sense of the world; they helped us know what to expect, so that each time we faced a new person or thing, we weren't starting all over again from scratch.

But stereotypes become dangerous when we continue to hold onto our mental images despite new evidence. (For instance, as a child you may have decided that all dogs bite—

Four Characteristics of Prejudice

1. a feeling of superiority
2. a feeling that the minority is different and alien
3. a feeling of rightful claim to power, privilege, and status
4. a fear and suspicion that the minority wants to take the power, privilege, and status from the dominant group

which means that when faced by friendly, harmless dogs, you assume they're dangerous and so you miss out on getting to know all dogs.) Stereotypes are particularly dangerous and destructive when they're directed at persons or groups of persons. That's when they turn into prejudice.

RACISM

Racism is treating members of a certain "race" differently because you think they're not as good, simply because they belong to that race. You might say that prejudice is the root of racism. Scientists aren't convinced that race is real, though. People are more alike than they're different, no matter what color their skin is or what continent their ancestors came from. In fact, scientists tell us that the idea of race is pretty much only useful as a medical concept— some groups of people from various parts of the world are more likely to get some illnesses than others, and some may respond better to certain medications.

Muslims aren't a separate race; they practice a certain religion. But race and racism get mixed up in conversations and ideas about Muslims. A lot of people tend to think of Muslims as Arab or Middle Eastern. Arabic could be considered an ethnicity or a race. We don't really know how to classify these people sometimes. Race is never black and white, but we tend to easily clump all people from Africa or African ancestry into the category of "black" and people from Latin America into "Latino," and so on. We don't know what to call Arabs and Middle Easterners, but we often treat them as a separate category of people, not just because of their religion. Lots of times prejudice is based on ignorance! We don't really know or understand the group of people we're judging.

A History Lesson

Muslims have been in North America a lot longer than most people might think. Unfortunately, prejudice aimed at Muslims has been here just as long.

THE HISTORY OF ISLAM

The most important historical figure in Islam is Mohammed. Beginning in 610 CE, Mohammed began receiving messages from God in Mecca (in present day Saudi Arabia). Eventually,

The Five Pillars of Islam

Muslims must follow five main pillars, or actions that are required of believers. These pillars are ideals, and aren't always followed by everyone. They are:

- *Declaring Faith (Shahadah):* Muslims must recite a testimony when they pray, and new converts to Islam must also say (in Arabic): "There is no God but Allah and Muhammad is His Messenger."
- *Prayer (Salah):* Five times a day, Muslims must pray in order to communicate with God. There is some flexibility in when and how often prayers are said.
- *Fasting (Zakah):* During the month of Ramadan, Muslims fast from dawn until dusk. Fasting is supposed to bring worshipers closer to God.
- *Charity (Sawm):* Devout Muslims are expected to give money to people in need.
- *Pilgrimage (Hajj):* Every Muslim who is able should travel to Mecca on pilgrimage.

The messages Mohammed received from God are written in the Qur'an.

he and his followers wrote down all the messages, which became the Qur'an, Muslims' holy scripture. Muslims believe that Mohammed was the last **prophet**, but they also think that other prophets existed, like Abraham and Jesus.

Mohammed and his followers were forced to move to a new city called Medina. From there, the new faith grew fast. After Mohammed died, his followers started to disagree about who should lead them. One group was the Sunnis and the other was the Shiites, a division within Islam that still exists today.

These days, Islam can be found all over the world. There are lots of Muslims in the Middle East, in northern Africa, and in southern Asia. In addition, Muslims have immigrated to the Americas, Europe, Eastern Asia, and other places around the world. It truly is a world religion.

EARLY IMMIGRANTS

The very first Muslims in North America were brought as slaves from Africa. While these unwilling immigrants brought Islam to the new homes, most of them eventually lost their religion.

A group of Muslim immigrants from the early 1900s.

Historical records speak of Muslims in the United States from time to time. But for a while, there were few Muslim immigrants coming to this country. Slowly, more and more Muslim immigrants came from various countries, for the same reasons as other immigrants. They wanted better lives here. They couldn't find jobs or live decent lives back home, so they set out on a journey to a new country.

Lots of those immigrants headed to the Midwest, where there was plenty of land for the taking. No one is positive where or when the first U.S. **mosque** was built. It may have been built in 1921, in Detroit, to serve as a place of prayer for the many Muslims that worked in the automobile industry at the time. Other reports suggest that the first mosque was built in North Dakota in 1929, to serve a small community of Lebanese Muslims that had moved into the area.

That first wave of Muslim immigrants came mostly from Syria and Lebanon. After World War I, the United States made it harder for all immigrants to come here, though, including Muslim immigrants. Then, after World War II, another wave of Muslim immigrants came, this time from places like Palestine, Egypt, and Eastern Europe. Many were educated and were escaping from religious or political **oppression**.

BLACKS AND ISLAM

In the 1900s, many black North Americans started **converting** to Islam. In part, they thought that the Islamic faith reconnected them with their Muslim ancestors who had been brought as slaves to the United States. And with the growing

For some blacks, Islam is a way to connect with their roots.

numbers of Arabic and South Asian Muslims, blacks in North America were now coming into more contact with the religion of Islam.

In 1930, a group of African Americans founded the Lost-Found Nation of Islam in Detroit. A few years later, a man named Elijah Muhammad took over its leadership. Muhammad believed in black superiority. He taught that blacks should be separate from whites and that they should stop believing in Christianity, which he said was a white person's religion.

Malcolm X was a follower of these beliefs. He was a great speaker and a very **controversial** figure. When he was assassinated, his son took over and made African American Islam both more **mainstream** and more in line with the rest of the Islamic world. Another leader, Louis Farrakhan, wanted the group to remain **radical**. He formed the Nation of Islam, which carried on the Lost-Found Nation's original beliefs. Over time, however, the Nation of Islam also became more mainstream.

A 2009 study found that black Americans made up 35 percent of all Muslim Americans. Today, there are some tensions between African American Muslims and Muslims of other backgrounds, but there are also many who are trying to bring the two sides of the same religion together.

How Many Muslims Are There?

- In Canada, in 2011, there were nearly 1 million Muslims, 2.8 percent of the total Canadian population. By 2030, experts predict that there will be triple that number of Muslims in Canada.

- In the United States, in 2011, there were about 2.5 million Muslims, which is less than 1 percent of the total American population. By 2030, experts predict that there will be about 6 million Muslim in the United States.

- About 16 million Muslims lived in the European Union in 2011, and that number is predicted to double by 2020. By 2050, one in five Europeans are likely to be Muslim, and by 2100, Muslims may make up one-quarter of Europe's people.

- In 2010, there were about 1.6 billion Muslims in the entire world. Experts predict that by 2030, there will be about 2.2 billion Muslims, which will be more than a quarter of the world's entire population.

Recent Immigration

Muslims immigrants from around the world continue to make their way to North America. Recent conflicts in the Middle East and in South Asia have made people flee their homelands and move elsewhere. The 1978 Soviet war in Afghanistan, 1979 revolution in Iran, and current day conflicts in Afghanistan and Iraq have all contributed to the flow of Muslim immigrants.

All sorts of Muslims have moved to the United States. They come from many different countries, and belong to different **sects** of Islam. Some are **devout** Muslims and some only practice their religion occasionally. Some are educated and others are not. But all are hoping for a better future in the United States.

September 11 and Beyond

When Islamic terrorists attacked the United States people all around the world were scared, angry, and sad. The September 11 attacks were organized by a group of foreign **militant** and fundamentalist Muslims who didn't like what the United States was doing in the Middle East. The terrorists had nothing to do with either Muslim Americans or the vast majority of foreign

Muslims. Immediately after September 11, many Muslim organizations around the world **denounced** the attacks.

But after the attacks, people started confusing the Islamic terrorists with all Muslims. Many people, both in North America and in other parts of the world, began to suspect anyone who was Muslim of being a terrorist. Fear and suspicion spread, and prejudice toward Muslims grew. Sadly, many law-abiding and peaceful Muslims suffered during the aftermath of September 11. People shouted obscenities on the street. People who looked like they might be Muslim or Arabic were stopped by police more often than other people, and were more often subject to heightened airport security searches.

And the fear of Muslims didn't go away as the years passed. In February of 2008, Muslim worshippers in Columbia, Tennessee, were heartbroken and frightened when their mosque was firebombed. Luckily, no one was injured, but the small mosque burned to the ground. A Muslim-owned business in Minnesota was also firebombed. Members of a **white-supremacist** group called Christian Identity were responsible for both incidents.

Later that year, other mosques in Nebraska, Maryland, and Illinois were also attacked. Death threats were mailed to the

Washington-based Council on American-Islamic Relations (CAIR) and to a Muslim candidate for the Irvine, California, city council. In Kansas, a "Molotov cocktail" was thrown at a Muslim walking down the street. And on the night of the presidential election in November, a group of white men jumped out of the shadows at a Muslim teenager as he walked along the street near his home in Staten Island, New York. They beat him and left him lying on the sidewalk. Apparently, they were angry that Barack Obama—a man they perceived to be a Muslim, though he is not—had been elected president.

Today, studies and surveys consistently show that Americans feel the most prejudice toward Muslims, out of all religious groups. A 2010 Gallup Center survey reported that 43 percent of Americans polled admitted to feeling at least "a little" prejudice toward Muslims. Only 18 percent said the same for Christians. Fifteen percent said the same for Jews, and 14 percent for Buddhists. The same survey showed that 31 percent of Americans said their view of Islam was "not favorable at all."

Unfortunately, some people don't only feel prejudiced against Muslims on the inside. They also take actions that prove it. An Abu Dhabi Gallup Center poll in 2011 showed

Muslims in Europe

Muslim immigrants in other parts of the world face the same, or worse, prejudice as they do in North America. Muslims represent one of the main groups of immigrants moving to countries such as Spain, France, and Italy. They are bringing a new culture with them, which frightens many Europeans. In response, some countries have passed harsh laws that prevent Muslims from practicing their culture or religion freely. For example, in 2011, France banned women from wearing the niqab, or face veil. The French claimed it was for security reasons, and because it wants to ensure women's rights. It's a very complicated issue, but prejudice and racism play big part in moves such as this one.

that almost half of all American Muslims had "personally experienced racial or religious discrimination." That could be anything from verbal attacks to vandalism to unfair treatment by the police.

Terrorism is a scary thing. The United States, Canada, the European Union, and other countries around the world are fighting hard to protect us all against terrorists. But terrorism and Islam are *not* the same thing. Most Muslims are good citizens of the countries where they live. They work hard and contribute to our world. They believe in God, and they get along with the people around them. They are not to blame for terrorism.

Does Islam Condone Terrorism?

According to Islamic tradition, "He who gives his life for an Islamic cause will have his sins forgiven and a place reserved in paradise." Many Muslims, however, insist that Islam forbids terrorism. One Islam expert explains that "fighting oppression is commendable . . . [but] harming innocent bystanders, even in times of war, was forbidden by the Prophet Muhammad."

CHAPTER 3

Real-Life Stories

Muslims in North America today face prejudice all the time. Although many are ordinary people who fit into their communities, they find themselves the target of occasional or even frequent prejudice, discrimination, and hatred. Here are some of their stories.

ANAN AMERI

Anan Ameri is a community leader in her city, a Muslim of Palestinian and Syrian descent, making her an Arab Muslim.

The Arab American National Museum works to show the contributions and culture of Arabs and Muslims, both in the United States and around the world.

As the sharp scissor suddenly cut through the taut red ribbon, Anan exhaled loudly and finally. May 5, 2005, was a proud day for Anan as the Arab American National Museum opened its doors to the public and all her years of hard work and devotion were finally realized. Anan Ameri is the director and co-founder of the Arab American National Museum in Dearborn, Michigan, the only museum in the United States devoted entirely to Arab Americans.

Anan was born in Damascus, Syria, as was her mother. Her father was born in Jafa, Palestine, in 1911 (before it became Israel). Anan spent her childhood in Syria, Jerusalem, and Jordan, where she earned her undergraduate degree. She earned her master's degree in Cairo and then lived in Beirut, Lebanon, before immigrating to the United States. Anan continued her education in the United States, earning a PhD in sociology from Wayne State University and becoming a visiting scholar in Middle Eastern Studies at Harvard University.

Today, Anan considers herself part of both the American world and the Arab world. Although she has lived in several Arab countries, she has called United States "home" for the past thirty years. As Anan puts it, "Being an Arab American means to me that I belong to both cultures, and cherish both." Anan is an American citizen but she keeps in close touch with her family in the Arab world and visits them often. Anan is proud to be an Arab American and has taken part in many positive organizations that promote the Arab community.

Anan explains why she has dedicated her career to this cause. "The more I realize the extent to which stereotyping of Arabs and Muslims has been part of American popular culture, and the more Arabs and Muslims are attacked, and portrayed

Anan Ameri works hard to fight prejudice and discrimination against Muslim Americans.

negatively, the more I feel I need to find ways to educate the public about the life, history, and culture as well as the contributions of Arabs and Muslim Americans, and to build institutions such as the Arab American National Museum, that addresses these issues."

In addition to being the cofounder and director of the Arab American National Museum, Anan has been the current cultural arts director of the Arab Community Center for Economics and Social Services (ACCESS) and the previous director of the Palestine Aid Society of America. She is an active participant in community events and a board member for various Arab organizations. She has also published numerous articles and essays on the Arab culture, as well as several books.

Anan also actively participates in many women's causes and organizations. She says, "I am a Palestinian/Syrian woman, and there is a lot of stereotyping in this country about Arab and Muslim women. . . . This negative image had a lot to do with the choices I made while living in America."

Many non-Muslim have a stereotype in their heads that all Muslim women are **subservient**, uneducated, and unliberated—but Anan proves that stereotype wrong. She is a highly educated and successful Muslim woman who has served in many leadership roles throughout her career. Anan is a proud example of a modern Muslim American woman. She is an incredible role model for us all of someone who has used her talents, energy, and intelligence to improve her community.

ASSIA AND IMAN BOUNDAOUI

Sisters Assia and Iman Boundaoui grew up outside Chicago, their lives straddling what it is to be Muslim and American.

The effects of prejudice are particularly hard on children.

Born to Algerian parents, they attended an Islamic school and a Sunni mosque around the corner from their home. They watched Nickelodeon and Al Jazeera. They got takeout food from Kentucky Fried Chicken and the falafel place down the street.

Assia, who is twenty, and Iman, who is eighteen, told NPR what it means to dress differently because of their religion, and how they are perceived by non-Muslims. "I'm proud to be Algerian, but it makes me mad when people think just because you have a scarf on, you can't be American," said Assia. "You know, they have to ask you, 'Where are you *really* from? No, no, where are you *really* from?'"

Few North Americans of European descent would face this question. No one cares much whether someone's ancestors came from England or the Netherlands, France or Germany— but Muslims are often thought of as being separate from the rest of the population, even if they were born and grew up in North America.

"In America, we would say we're Muslim first, because that's what makes us different, I guess," Assia told NPR. "So you identify with that one factor within you that stands out. But in another country, like in a Muslim country, and someone asks us to identify ourselves, we would say we're American."

Prejudice Against Muslims Around the World

A recent study asked people from 19 European countries plus Canada and the United States whether they would be willing to have a Muslim as their neighbor.

- Canada was the least prejudiced: only 6.5 percent said they wouldn't want to live next door to a Muslim.
- The United States came next: 10.9 percent would be unwilling to have a Muslim for a neighbor.
- Next in line was the UK, where 14.1 percent said they wouldn't want to live next to a Muslim.
- The highest levels of prejudice were in Finland (18.9% said they would not want to have a Muslim for a neighbor), Norway (19.3%), Belgium (19.8%), and Greece (20.9%).

Iman told NPR that she felt most American during a trip to Paris she took as a high school senior. Her group visited a Muslim school that was opened in response to a law banning religious headwear in public schools.

"We were talking to the girls and they were crying and telling us that before the school was made, the girls there had to make the choice of not going to school or attending school without the scarf," Iman said. "It was probably the hardest decision they've ever had to make. And me and my friends were looking at them and at that moment were like, 'Thank God we live in America, that I can walk down the street with my scarf on without having to decide to take it off because I have to go to school.'"

Assia and Iman's story tells us something important about the United States. Prejudice and misunderstandings are all too common in America.

But at the same time, laws based on freedom and tolerance protect both Muslim Americans and Muslim Canadians. North America has high **ideals**. Now we just need to find ways to live up to those ideals!

Fighting Prejudice

The United States used to be called a melting pot. This expression meant that people of different religions, races, and ethnic backgrounds had all come together in America, including millions of Muslims. Today, many people think that "melting pot" is the wrong **metaphor** to use for the United States, because it implies that all these different kinds of people cooked down into a single "stew," losing their individual characteristics. Nowadays, people speak instead of the United States as a salad bowl or a mosaic—something where all the separate pieces hold on to what makes them different and special, and yet all of them contribute to something bigger, the thing that makes America what it is today.

Americans, no matter their backgrounds, share some very important beliefs. They believe in democracy, in freedom of speech, and in the right for a person to worship as she chooses. These common beliefs give Americans an important foundation on which to come together. They give Americans something to work toward, despite their differences.

President Woodrow Wilson once said that America is not set apart from other countries "so much by its wealth and

Canada and Human Rights

Canada started out with less emphasis on human rights than the United States had. However, in 1948, the Canadian government signed the Universal Declaration of Human Rights, which guaranteed rights for all people under Canadian law. Since then, most Canadians have worked hard to live up to these high ideals. Canada has a reputation for being a tolerant society—but prejudice and discrimination do still exist in Canada.

power as by the fact that it was born with an ideal, a purpose." The United States was created to be a nation where the people rule themselves, where everyone has certain rights, regardless of their religion, the color of their skin, their gender, or how

President Woodrow Wilson

much money they have. Reality doesn't always live up to these high ideals, unfortunately—but those ideals give Americans a goal to work toward as a country.

Human Rights Laws in Europe

The European Union (EU) states that "human dignity, freedom, democracy, equality, the rule of law and respect for human rights are the values" on which it is founded. Fighting discrimination and prejudice is one of the EU's top priorities, and it has committed billions of euros to the battle over the next few years.

AMERICA'S BATTLE AGAINST PREJUDICE

At the very beginning of the United States, when the thirteen original colonies first declared their independence from England on July 4, 1776, they stated that all "are created equal, that they are endowed by their Creator with certain

unalienable rights, that among them are Life, Liberty, and the pursuit of happiness."

America's history is the story of how it has worked to live up to these ideals. Near the end of the American Civil War, President Abraham Lincoln expressed his belief in the nation's central ideal of freedom for all: "It is not merely for today, but for all time to come. . . . The nation is worth fighting for, to secure such an inestimable jewel." The Civil War was mostly about ending slavery, but the ideas that Americans began to think about then affected other groups' later struggles against prejudice, including Muslims.

In 1866, the **Civil Rights** Act won a small victory in the battle against prejudice, stating that "all persons shall have the same rights . . . to make and enforce contracts, to sue, be parties, give evidence, and to the full and equal benefit of all laws." Then, in 1868, the 14th Amendment made still deeper inroads in the legal battle to live up to America's ideals. This amendment stated that "all persons born or **naturalized** in the United States . . . are citizens . . . nor shall any State deprive any person of life, liberty, or property, without **due process of law**; nor deny to any person . . . the equal protection of the laws."

These changes to American laws were important steps in the fight against prejudice—but in real life, most Muslims

President Lyndon B. Johnson signs the 1964 Civil Rights Act as Martin Luther King, Jr., and others, look on.

and other minorities still faced prejudice every day. The Civil Rights Movement of the 1960s continued the struggle, and another major victory was won in 1964, when the Civil Rights Act was passed. It prohibited employment discrimination based on race, religion, sex, or national origin. Part of the act, Title VI, also made public access discrimination against the law. Another part of the Civil Rights Act, Title VIII, was the first federal fair housing law. In other words, landlords and realtors couldn't refuse to let someone rent or buy a house because of who they were. This law was added to in 1988, and the Civil Rights Act of 1991 also added to Title VII protections, including the right to a jury trial. Many of these laws were aimed at African Americans, but Muslims and other minorities benefited from them as well.

Today, America is doing a much better job at living up to its ideals than it did two hundred years ago, a hundred years ago, or even fifty years ago. Laws are a good way to protect people's rights and fight prejudice. But in the twenty-first-century, Muslim Americans present the United States with new challenges to their ideals.

In 2011, there was a congressional hearing on the civil rights of American Muslims. Senator Dick Durbin from Illinois said he convened the hearing because of rising Islamophobia—prejudice against Muslims—that had become evident in the United States with Qur'an burnings, **hate speech**, and restrictions on building mosques.

"We should all agree that it is wrong to blame an entire community for the wrongdoing of a few," said Durbin, referring to Americans who blame all Muslims for terrorists' actions. "Guilt by association is not the American way."

Durbin's star witness was Thomas Perez, the Justice Department's assistant attorney general for civil rights. Since the terrorist attacks of 9/11, Perez said he has seen a "steady stream of violence and discrimination" against Muslims, Arabs, **Sikhs**, and South Asians in the United States. "In each city and town where I have met with leaders of these communities, I have been struck by the sense of fear that pervades their lives—fear of violence, **bigotry** and hate."

Perez reported that since 9/11, the Justice Department has investigated more than 800 incidents of violence, vandalism, and arson against people suspected of being Muslim. He also noted that Muslim complaints about workplace discrimination have increased by 150 percent since 9/11. Although Muslims make up less than 2 percent of the United States population, they accounted for about one-quarter of the 3,386 religious discrimination claims filed during the previous year. Complaints filed by Jews rose slightly during the same period, while complaints filed by Catholics and Protestants declined. Claims of race, sex, and age discrimination also fell.

Muslim children are harassed at school, Perez said. They're called "terrorists" and told to "go home." Muslim students form the largest category of religious discrimination cases handled by the Department of Justice's education division. "Parents worry, 'Will my child be next?'" said Farhana Khera, executive director of Muslim Advocates, who also testified.

Other members of the Senate, meanwhile, agreed that Muslims' rights should be protected, but many spoke up to insist that "there are two sides to this story." "Efforts to **recruit** and **radicalize** young Muslims must be dealt with," said Senator Lindsey Graham of South Carolina. "To the American Muslim community, I will stand with you, but you will have to help your country," he said. "Get in this fight and protect your young people and your nation from radicalization." And Senator Jon Kyl of Arizona insisted, "The only way to stop terrorists is to recognize where they are coming from. Political correctness cannot stand in the way of identifying those who would do us harm."

Fear is often a large part of prejudice. During World War II, for example, when the United States was at war with Japan, Japanese Americans were suspected and feared by other Americans. Many were even sent to **concentration camps**. This same sense of justified fear and the need to protect ourselves often lies behind anti-Islam discrimination and prejudice today.

Sociologists who study prejudice say that scapegoating is often part of what makes people fear and hate another

Fighting Prejudice   51

group of people. Because people are frustrated and scared, they blame a group of people for their problems. This helps people feel more in control. In other words, if we can point to a particular group of people we can recognize and say, "There's the problem! Those people are the enemy!" then maybe we will be able to fight and overcome them. We can take action against them. We can band together and be brave and overcome evil.

But no group of people is ever completely evil—and we can never assume that because someone is Muslim he is also a terrorist who means us harm. In times of fear, however, it

Getting to know people is one of the best ways to overcome prejudice.

becomes more difficult to live out the ideals that are built into our government's laws.

That's because ultimately, prejudice is something that lives inside people. No law can change the way a person thinks about others. That's something we each have to do. The battle we have to fight is inside our own minds. We fight for a better world by changing the way we talk and act. We do it by changing the way we think.

CELEBRATING DIVERSITY

One of the first things that has to change is the way we think about differences. Instead of being frightened of the ways people are different from ourselves, we need to start feeling curious and interested. We need to be willing to learn from people who are different. We need to enjoy the differences!

Most people enjoy **diversity** when it comes to the world around them. They like different kinds of food. They read different kinds of books. They enjoy different kinds of music and television shows. The world would be pretty boring if everything was exactly the same!

People are also diverse, in the same way as the rest of the world is. Although all of us feel the same basic emotions—sadness and happiness, anger and laughter, loneliness and pride, jealousy and compassion, to name just a few—and most of us have pretty much the same structure—a head, a body, arms and legs—we also are different in many ways. Our hair, eyes, and skin come in different colors. Our noses are big or little or something in between. Our bodies are different sizes and shapes. And when you get down to the details—to our fingerprints and the DNA inside our cells—we're absolutely unique, despite all the things we have in common with other human beings. Each of us looks at the world a little differently. We believe different things. And we offer different things as well.

The world is a richer place because of all this human diversity. You can learn from and enjoy your friends because, although they're like you in some ways, they're also different from you in other ways. Those differences make them interesting! And in a similar way, we can learn from human beings' different languages, different music, different ways of thinking about God, different lifestyles.

Prejudice, however, focuses on the differences in a negative way. It doesn't value all that differences have to offer us. Instead, it divides people into in-groups and out-groups. It breaks the Golden Rule.

Do you recognize prejudice when you hear it? Sometimes it's hard. We get so used to certain ways of thinking that we

What Is the Golden Rule?

"Treat others the way you want to be treated." It's the most basic of all human moral laws—and it's been found in all religions and all cultures for thousands of years. The earliest record of this principle is in the Code of Hammurabi, written nearly 4,000 years ago. About 2,500 years ago, Confucius, the great Chinese philosopher, wrote, "Never impose on others what you would not choose for yourself." An ancient Egyptian papyrus contains a similar thought: "That which you hate to be done to you, do not do to another." Ancient Greek philosophers wrote, "Do not do to others what would anger you if done to you by others." An early Buddhist teacher expressed a similar concept: "Just as I am so are they, just as they are so am I." Jesus Christ, whom Christians follow, said, "Do unto others as you would have them do unto you." The Prophet Mohammed, whose teachings Muslims follow, said, "As you would have people do to you, do to them; and what you dislike to be done to you, don't do to them," as well as, "That which you seek for yourself, seek for all humans."

You can't follow this ancient rule and practice prejudice. The Golden Rule and prejudice are not compatible!

become blind to what's really going on. But anytime you hear people being lumped together, chances are prejudice is going on. Statements like these are all signs of prejudice:

Poor kids smell bad.
Girls run funny.
Old people are boring.
Special ed kids are weird.
Jocks are jerks.

Rather than building bridges between people, prejudice puts up walls. It makes it hard to talk to others or understand them. And those walls can lead to hatred, violence, and even wars.

A first step to ending prejudice is speaking up against it whenever you hear it. Point it out when you hear your friends or family being prejudiced. They may not even realize that's what they're being.

But even more important, you need to spot prejudice when it's inside you. That's not always easy, of course. Here are some ways experts suggest you can fight prejudice when you find it inside yourself:

Building Understanding

Although most Muslims are not terrorists, some fundamentalist Muslims do in fact support terrorism. How should we react to people like that? Is it prejudice to hate and fear people who truly wish us harm?

The ancient Chinese treatise called *The Art of War* counsels that victory is built on knowing both our enemy and ourselves. Many Middle East experts say we need to build a better understanding of what fuels terrorists' violence if we are to effectively fight it. By doing so, they claim, we can work to build societies where young people are not willing to give their lives to terrorism, where better economic conditions mean that people have less to be angry about, where laws protect the rights of all groups of people, and where all groups have a voice, allowing open dialogues between people who are now enemies.

When people know they will be heard and their concerns addressed, they are less likely to resort to violence. Prejudice, fear, and hatred lead to more violence, which in turn leads to more prejudice, fear, and hatred. It's a vicious cycle. Somebody has to stop the cycle!

1. Learn more about groups of people who are different from you. Read books about their history; read fiction that allows you to walk in their shoes in your imagination; watch movies that portray them accurately.

2. Get to know people who are different from you. Practice being a good listener, focusing on what they have to say rather than on your own opinions and experiences. Ask about others' backgrounds and family stories.

3. Practice compassion. Imagine what it would feel like to be someone who is different from you. Your imagination is a powerful tool you can use to make the world better!

What does it all come down to in the end? Perhaps the war against prejudice can best be summed up with just two words: communication and respect.

Find Out More

In Books

Abdo, Geneive. *Mecca and Main Street: Muslim Life in America After 9/11*. New York: Oxford University Press, 2006.

Curtis, Edward E. IV. *Muslims in America: A Short History.* New York: Oxford University Press, 2009.

Ebrahimji, Maria M. and Zahra T. Suratwala. *I Speak for Myself: American Women on Being Muslim.* Ashland, Ore: White Cloud Press, 2011.

On the Internet

ISLAM

www.pbs.org/empires/islam

MUSLIM STEREOTYPES

www.tolerance.org/activity/debunking-muslim-myths

PBS GLOBAL CONNECTIONS

www.pbs.org/wgbh/globalconnections/index.html

GLOSSARY

bigotry: Intolerance toward those who have different opinions from oneself.

civil rights: The rights of a citizen to personal and political freedom under the law.

concentration camps: Places where large numbers of political prisoners are held, especially during times of war.

conservative: Holding on to traditional values and cautious about making changes.

controversial: Causing arguments.

converting: Persuading someone to make a change in his or her religious beliefs.

denounced: Publicly declared to be wrong.

devout: Deeply committed to one's religion.

diversity: Being different in lots of different ways.

due process of law: Fair treatment through the court system. In other words, no one can be simply hauled away and thrown in prison without a trial and other legal protection.

effeminate: Possessing feminine qualities; usually applied to males in a negative way.

hate speech: Communication that carries no meaning other than the expression of hatred for some group of people.

ideals: Ideas about what is perfect.

liberal: Open to new ideas that support social change.

mainstream: Having to do with the ideas, attitudes, and activities that are considered to be normal by most of the people in a society.

metaphor: A figure of speech where something is used to symbolize something else.

militant: Having to do with an aggressive support of a particular viewpoint; being willing to take violent action in support of that view.

mosque: A Muslim place of worship.

naturalized: Became a citizen despite having been born in another country.

prophet: An inspired religious teacher who teaches about God.

radical: Extreme.

radicalize: To persuade someone to accept extreme perspectives on reforming the world.

recruit: To persuade someone to join a group.

sects: Smaller religious groups whose views differ in some way from that of the larger religion to which they belong.

Sikhs: Members of a religion that started in northern India in the sixteenth century. Sikhs believe in one God. They also believe in a cycle of reincarnation from which humans can free themselves by living righteous lives as active members of society.

sociologists: People who study the way groups of humans behave.

subservient: Prepared to obey others without question.

unalienable: Having to do with something that cannot be separated or taken away

Western: Having to do with the civilization of Europe and the countries (the United States, Australia, Canada, etc.) most influenced by Europe.

white supremacy: The belief that white people are better than others and that they should dominate and control the world.

BIBLIOGRAPHY

Allawi, Ali A. *The Occupation of Iraq: Winning the War, Losing the Peace.* New Haven, N.J.: Yale University Press, 2007.

Associated Press. "Poll Shows U.S. Views on Muslim-Americans." December 17, 2004. www.msnbc.msn.com/id/6729916.

Curtis, Edward E. IV. "Five Myths about Mosques in America." *The Washington Post.* 29 August 2010. www.washingtonpost.com/wp-dyn/content/article/2010/08/26/AR2010082605510.html.

Gallup Center for Muslim Studies. "In U.S. Religious Prejudice Stronger Against Muslims." *GallupWellbeing.* 21 January 2010. www.gallup.com/poll/125312/religious-prejudice-stronger-against-muslims.aspx.

Ghazali, Abdus Sattar. "Muslim Immigration to the USA." *American Muslim Perspective.* 1 January 2004. www.amp.ghazali.net/html/four_waves.html.

"Half of U.S. Muslims Face Prejudice." PressTV. 3 August 2011. www.gallup.com/poll/125312/religious-prejudice-stronger-against-muslims.aspx.

"Mosques of America: Ross, North Dakota." IIP Digital. iipdigital.usembassy.gov/st/english/inbrief/2011/07/20110729165008su0.1452557.html#axzz1rAvsnhgE.

The Pew Forum on Religion & Public Life. "The Future of the Global Muslim Population." January 2011. features.pewforum.org/muslim-population-graphic/#/United%20States.

Simons, Rae. *The World Gone Mad.* Broomall, Penn: Mason Crest Publishers, 2009.

Sun Tzu. *The Art of War.* Translated from the Chinese with Introduction and Critical Notes by Lionel Giles, first published in 1910, available at www.kimsoft.com/polwar.htm.

TeachMideast. "Stereotypes of Arabs, Middle Easterners and Muslims." www.teachmideast.org/essays/26-stereotypes/38-stereotypes-of-arabs-middle-easterners-and-muslims.

Tweed, Thomas A. "Islam in America: From African Slaves to Malcolm X." National Humanities Center. December 2004. nationalhumanitiescenter.org/tserve/twenty/tkeyinfo/islam.htm.

U.S. Whitehouse. "National Strategy for Combating Terrorism." Washington, D.C., 2003. www.whitehouse.gov/news/releases/2003/02/counter_terrorism/counter_terrorism_strategy.pdf

Woodruff, Judy. "Young Muslim Americans Struggle with Identity." *NPR*. 14 September 2006. www.npr.org/templates/story/story.php?storyId=6071738.

INDEX

Ameri, Anan 33–38

Boundaoui, Assie and
    Iman 38–40

Christian 8, 9, 12, 25, 28,
    29, 55
Civil Rights Act 47–49
Council on American-Islamic
    Relations (CAIR) 28, 29

ethnocentrism 17

immigrants 22, 23, 27, 30

Malcolm X 25
Muhammad 9, 20, 25, 31

prophet 9, 21, 31, 55

Qur'an 8, 9, 21, 49

racism 10, 16, 17, 20

September 11th 27, 28
stereotype 11, 13–16, 37

terrorism 9, 13, 30, 31, 43, 57

Picture Credits

About the Author

Ellyn Sanna is the author of hundreds of books for children, young adults, and adults. She has also worked for many years as an editor and small-business owner.